## PICTURE LIBRARY

# BIRDS OF PREY

# PICTURE LIBRARY

# BIRDS OF PREY

## Norman Barrett

## Franklin Watts

### New York   London   Sydney   Toronto

©1991 Franklin Watts

Franklin Watts, Inc.
387 Park Avenue South
New York, NY 10016

Printed in the United Kingdom

Library of Congress Cataloging-in-Publication Data

Barrett, Norman S.
    Birds of prey/Norman Barrett.
        p. cm. — (Picture library)
    Includes index
    Summary: A look at such predatory birds as eagles, vultures, and
owls and how their hunting methods differ.
    ISBN 0-531-14151-9
    1. Birds of prey — Juvenile literature. [1. Birds of prey.
2. Predatory animals.]
I. Title. II. Series.
QL696.F3B37 1991
598.9'1—dc20                                                    90-46306
                                                                CIP AC

**Designed by**
Barrett and Weintroub

**Research by**
Deborah Spring

**Picture Research by**
Ruth Sonntag

**Photographs by**
Survival Anglia (pages 2-27, 30
    bottom, back cover)
N.S. Barrett (pages 29, 30 top &
    left)
Colourview Publications (page
    28)
Natural Science Photos/David
    Condon (cover)

**Illustration by**
Rhoda and Robert Burns

**Technical Consultant**
Michael Chinery

# Contents

# Introduction

Birds of prey have strong, hooked beaks and sharp, powerful claws. They eat flesh and prey mostly on other birds, small mammals, reptiles or fish.

△ An eagle soars high in the air searching the ground below for possible victims.

Eagles are among the largest birds of prey. Others include hawks, which are smaller members of the eagle family, falcons, vultures, and the not closely related owls. People who study birds call birds of prey "raptors."

The raptors have excellent eyesight and most of them are expert fliers. They use a variety of hunting methods.

Eagles and vultures soar high in the sky looking for prey on the ground. Eagles suddenly swoop down to catch their victims unaware. Vultures prey on dead animals and often circle around waiting for their victims to die. Some falcons catch their prey in the air. Owls hunt by night.

△A barn owl arrives back at its roost grasping its prey, a mouse caught in the fields.

7

# Looking at birds of prey

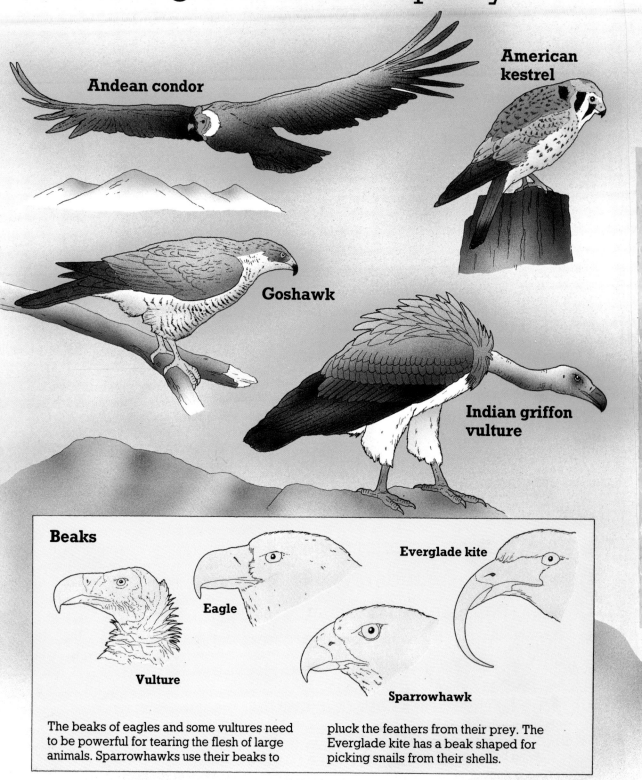

**Andean condor**

**American kestrel**

**Goshawk**

**Indian griffon vulture**

**Beaks**

**Vulture**

**Eagle**

**Everglade kite**

**Sparrowhawk**

The beaks of eagles and some vultures need to be powerful for tearing the flesh of large animals. Sparrowhawks use their beaks to pluck the feathers from their prey. The Everglade kite has a beak shaped for picking snails from their shells.

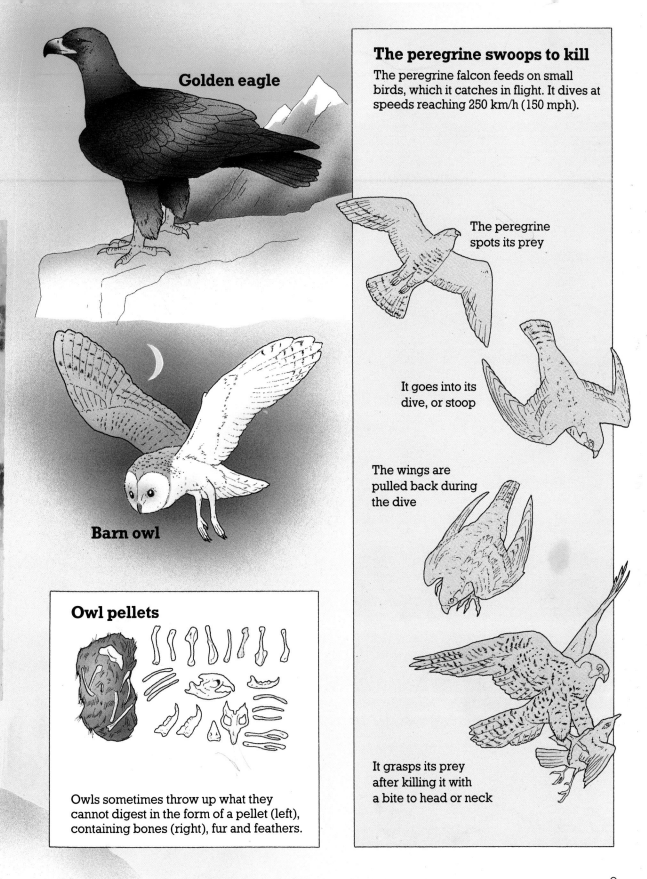

**Golden eagle**

**Barn owl**

## The peregrine swoops to kill

The peregrine falcon feeds on small birds, which it catches in flight. It dives at speeds reaching 250 km/h (150 mph).

The peregrine spots its prey

It goes into its dive, or stoop

The wings are pulled back during the dive

It grasps its prey after killing it with a bite to head or neck

## Owl pellets

Owls sometimes throw up what they cannot digest in the form of a pellet (left), containing bones (right), fur and feathers.

# Eagles

There are about 50 species (kinds) of eagle. They hunt only during the day. Golden eagles usually nest on high cliffs and defend large territories.

Eagles are found in most parts of the world. They eat a variety of food, depending on where they live. Their prey includes, snakes, lizards, birds and small mammals, even monkeys. They also eat carrion (rotting flesh). Bald eagles and some of the smaller eagles eat fish.

△ An African fish eagle swoops low over a lake to catch its prey.

▷ A bald eagle in its nest, or aerie, with its two chicks. Bald eagles get their name from their white head feathers, which give an appearance of baldness. They build their aeries near water, in the tops of tall trees. They are found only in North America, mostly in Alaska.

△ A short-toed eagle makes a meal of a snake. Most snake eagles have a dense covering of breast and leg feathers as protection against snake bites.

◁ A white-bellied sea eagle flies off with its prey. Sea eagles eat sea snakes as well as fish, grabbing their prey from water with their talons. They also prey on water birds and pick up food on land.

▷ The harpy eagle lives in the rainforests of South and Central America. It is the largest of all eagles, with a weight of about 8 kg (18 lb). It preys on mammals, especially capuchin monkeys.

▽ The bateleur eagle of Africa preys on anything from termites to monitor lizards. It often steals prey from other birds.

# Hawks and falcons

Many of the smaller raptors are called hawks or falcons. True hawks, often called accipiters, include the sparrowhawk and the goshawk. They have fairly short, rounded wings and long tails. They live mainly in wooded areas and feed chiefly on other birds.

Buteos, such as the common buzzard, are closely related to the accipiters, as are harriers and kites. All are often called hawks.

△ A Galapagos hawk in flight. This belongs to the buteo group of hawks and soars high like an eagle, using its excellent eyesight to spot prey on the ground.

Falcons belong to a separate family. They are long-winged, fast-flying birds that hunt mainly in open country. They include the peregrine, the merlin and several species of kestrels.

▽A goshawk feeds its chicks. The goshawk is an accipiter. Its short wings are not designed for soaring.

Hawks nest in trees, on cliffs or on the ground. They build their nests with grass and twigs.

Falcons never build nests. They lay their eggs in holes or scrape away a spot on a cliff or on the ground. Some take over old nests of other birds.

Hawks usually lay from one to three eggs, falcons from three to five. The young birds are ready to leave the nest and fend for themselves after 4 to 8 weeks.

△ Newly hatched merlin chicks in the nest with unhatched eggs. The merlin is a small falcon of northern lands. It hunts in open country, usually at ground level.

▷ A fledgling (young bird) harrier in a threatening pose. Harriers are found all over the world. These long-winged hawks hunt in open country, gliding slowly in search of small animals, especially rodents.

△ A common buzzard thrusts its talons forward to grasp its prey.

▷ A brahminy kite. Kites soar in great sweeping circles, and may be recognized by their forked tails.

◁ An osprey returns with a fish for its mate. Ospreys build their nests in trees near water. They are also called fishing hawks, but are not closely related to the other birds of prey.

△ The peregrine falcon is built for speed. It catches birds while in flight, swooping down from above. Falcons grasp their prey with their claws, but, unlike hawks, they make the kill with a bite to head or neck.

◁ The crested caracara is a long-legged falcon sometimes known as the Mexican eagle. Caracaras are found in South and Central America and, like vultures, feed on dead flesh.

# Vultures

Vultures are scavengers. They live on carrion. They circle the skies and move in for any leftovers of another animal's kill. Or they might wait for a sick or injured animal to die.

Vultures live on all continents except Australia and Antarctica. There are two families. New World vultures live in the Americas. Old World vultures, which belong to the same family as eagles, are found in Europe, Asia and Africa.

△ Vultures of the African savannah descend on a dead elephant, not the easiest of animals to feed on. The beaks and talons of some vultures are not strong enough to tear flesh until it has started to rot. Many vultures have bare necks and heads, so they do not get their feathers clogged with dried blood after feeding.

△ A Himalayan griffon vulture being mobbed (attacked) by ravens disputing a nesting site high up in the mountains.

◁ The king vulture, with its brilliantly colored head, lives in the rainforests of South and Central America.

# Owls

There are more than 130 species of owl. They are found in most parts of the world. They usually live alone and hunt at night.

Owls' feathers are soft and fluffy. These muffle the sound of the wing-beats in flying, so owls can pounce on their prey silently. Their hearing is especially good, and they can detect the slightest rustle in the grass. They feed mostly on small mammals such as rats and mice.

▽Barn owls make their nests in holes in trees or in dark places such as the roofs of barns. They are useful to farmers because they destroy pests such as rats and mice. Owls are easy to recognize because of the large round head with its ruff of feathers around the eyes. There are 10 species of barn owl. They belong to a different family from the other, so-called "typical," owls.

◁ A short-eared owl with its clutch of eggs in its nest on the ground. Most owls lay 3 or 4 eggs, but some species lay between 2 and 12.

▽ A great gray owl with its chicks. The great gray is one of the largest owls. Young owls are reared by both parents, and stay in the nest for longer than most other birds.

△ The long-eared owl
with its unmistakable
ear tufts. Some other
species of owl have
these tufts, also called
horns or ears. They are
not ears, but tufts of
feathers. The owls'
large ear openings are
covered by their facial
feathers.

▷ The snowy owl
breeds in the Arctic and
migrates south in the
winter. Unlike most
other owls, the snowy
owl is active during the
daytime.

# Secretary bird

A strange bird, not closely related to the other birds of prey, lives in the grasslands and sparsely wooded regions of Africa. It is called the secretary bird. It gets its name from the tufts of feathers on its head, which look like the quill pens once used by clerks.

The secretary bird has long legs, and prefers to run after its prey rather than fly. It feeds on insects, frogs and small reptiles.

△A secretary bird at its nest. These birds build huge nests of twigs from thorn trees. They have the hooked beak of an eagle, but strut around like storks.

# Survival

Like other animals, birds of prey become endangered when their habitats are destroyed or polluted.

Many birds of prey have been hunted by farmers, who regard them as pests. Egg collectors rob the nests of rare eagles and condors.

Most endangered species are now protected by law. But stricter regulations are needed to control the use of pesticides and the pollution of water by industrial waste.

△ The bald eagle, the national bird of the United States, has become an endangered species over all of the country except Alaska. It is now protected and in some places is reared in captivity before being set free in the wild.

# The story of birds of prey

### The first raptor

Birds, like mammals, developed from reptiles. Fossil evidence of the first known bird of prey, or raptor, comes from what is now the southwestern United States. This was a 2 meter (6–7 ft) tall ground-dwelling bird called Diatryma, which lived about 70 million years ago.

### Beaks and talons

Raptors are now found in all parts of the world except Antarctica. They developed their sharp talons for grasping their prey and their powerful hooked beaks for killing it and tearing at the flesh.

### Continuing evolution

As the evolution of birds continues, some other birds have developed some of the features or habits of raptors. Birds such as the shrike, for example, eat mice and young birds as well as insects. As a result, they are developing beaks with hooked tips.

Parrots and cockatoos do have beaks and claws like raptors. But they use their beaks for opening nuts and seeds and their claws for holding their food and climbing. One parrot, however, the kea of New Zealand, began eating flesh when sheep were introduced into the country by the first European settlers. Although it ate only the flesh of dead sheep, it was thought to be a killer, and was almost eradicated before it became a protected species. It now lives mainly in the mountainous areas of New Zealand's South Island, and is the only parrot in the world to be found at the snow-line.

△ The kea, a New Zealand mountain parrot that has developed vulturelike habits.

### Tamed hunters

People first began to use birds of prey for hunting more than 3,000 years ago, in both ancient China and Persia. Falcons were tamed and trained to kill and bring back birds and small mammals for the dining table. This hunting sport, called falconry or hawking, became popular in Europe and

△ Falconry was popular in Europe in the Middle Ages. It was a favorite sport of kings and nobles, and all the great households had one or more falconers.

△ A modern falconer demonstrates the art of falconry. Although birds of prey hunt to live, many people think that animals should not be killed in the name of sport.

southwestern Asia in the Middle Ages. Even eagles were used in some countries, to catch deer and large birds.

Falconry declined in the 1700s, when people began to use guns to shoot birds. But it still continues as a sport in some countries.

## The hunter hunted

When people began to use shotguns to kill game birds such as pheasants, their former "pets," the hawks and falcons, became unwanted competition. Other birds of prey, such as owls and eagles, which lived on animals required for the dining table – fish and small mammals as well as

birds – also became enemies. People now began to hunt these birds of prey. They shot them, trapped and poisoned them, and stole their eggs. Some raptors were wiped out completely from certain areas.

## Protection

In many places, laws have been brought in to protect birds of prey and save them from extinction. But many species are still threatened as pollution and destruction of their habitats continue to reduce their numbers.

# Facts and records

## Symbols

Civilizations, ancient and modern, have admired birds of prey as symbols of strength and bravery. The owl is regarded as a symbol of wisdom. Golden eagles figured on ensigns for the ancient kings of Babylon and Persia, and for Roman legions. North American Indians believed bald and golden eagles possessed magical powers. The bald eagle is the national symbol of the United States, the Andean condor that of Mexico.

△ A figure of an eagle tops an Indian totem pole in Canada.

## Tricky vulture

The Egyptian vulture is the smallest and weakest of the vultures. When vultures feed on a carcass, it is always last in line, feeding on tiny scraps of flesh left on the bones. Yet it is one of the few creatures that have learned how to use a tool. Its trick is to

△ The Egyptian vulture, one of the few creatures that can use a tool.

pick up a stone in its beak and then keep dropping it onto an ostrich egg until the shell breaks.

## The honey buzzard

The honey buzzard is poorly named. Although it does sometimes take honeycomb from bees' nests, it feeds mainly on wasp grubs. In addition, it is not even a true buzzard, being more closely related to the kites.

It also eats adult wasps after skillfully nipping off their stings.

△ A honey buzzard brings home a piece of wasp comb for its chicks.

# Glossary

**Accipiters**
Species of short-winged hawk that normally chase their prey through wooded country.

**Aerie**
The nest of a bird of prey, especially of an eagle.

**Buteos**
Species of hawk that usually soar high in the air and then swoop on their prey.

**Carcass**
The dead body of an animal.

**Carrion**
The rotting flesh of dead animals.

**Evolution**
The development and change of species, usually over millions of years.

**Extinction**
The dying out of a species, when there are no longer any living specimens.

**Falconry**
The sport of hunting small birds and other animals with hawks or falcons.

**Fledgling**
A young bird before growing its full crop of feathers.

**Fossil**
An impression of the remains of an ancient animal preserved in rock.

**Pollution**
The poisoning of air, water or food, usually by humans, by chemicals from industrial waste or by pesticides.

**Prey**
Creatures killed by others for food.

**Raptor**
A bird of prey.

**Scavenger**
A creature that lives on scraps left by others. Scavengers also clean up dung and whole dead animals.

**Species**
A particular kind of animal. Animals of the same species breed young of that species.

**Talons**
Sharp, curved claws.

# Index